CONTENTS

WAR AND WEAPONS

Brian Williams

Published 1979 by Warwick Press, 730 Fifth Avenue,
New York 10019
First published in Great Britain by Ward Lock in 1978
Copyright © 1978 by Grisewood & Dempsey Ltd
Printed in Italy by New Interlitho, Milan
6 5 4 3 2 1 All rights reserved

WARWICK PRESS · NEW YORK

Library of Congress Catalog Card No. 78–67838
ISBN 0–531–09132–5
ISBN 0–531–09117–1 lib. bdg.

R. Payne

Every Roman legion carried a standard. The standard on the left is decorated with images of Nero, Roman emperor A.D. 54–68, and his wife. It was carried into battle by a bearer dressed in a lion skin. It was a great disgrace for a legion to lose its standard.

dagger belt with sword

COH·II·PRI

standard bearer, 1st century A.D.

Praetorian in battle dress, 2nd century A.D.

javelin thrower, 2nd century B.C.

The Roman Army

The Romans had the best-trained army in the ancient world. They conquered and ruled a huge empire, winning many battles against their "barbarian" enemies.

The army was divided into legions of about 5,000 men. Each legion was divided into cohorts of 500 men, and each cohort was made up of centuries (companies of 100 men).

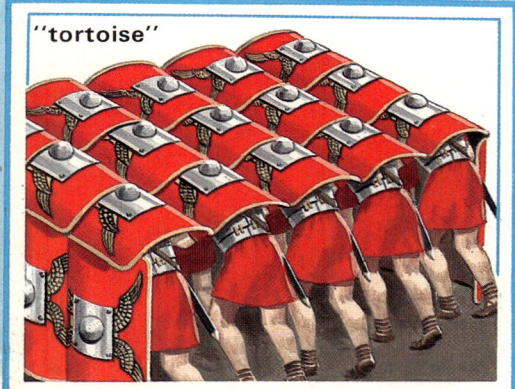

"tortoise"

The officer in charge of a century was called a centurion. All legionary soldiers were Roman citizens. They were tough, disciplined and well-paid.

There were also foreign troops called auxiliaries, including archers and cavalry. The auxiliaries usually guarded the frontiers, while the legions were kept in reserve, ready to march into battle.

The legions could travel long distances quickly along the fine Roman roads. With them went engineers, such as bridge-builders, and the artillery—catapults and other siege weapons. The soldiers set up camps surrounded by a ditch, earthen ramparts and high wooden fences.

Each soldier in the front lines wore a plumed metal helmet and body armor made of metal plates. He carried a curved shield, two javelins, a short stabbing dagger and a double-edged sword.

phalanx of legionaries, 2nd century B.C.

In battle, the legions used clever tactics. The soldiers advanced behind a wall of shields and threw their javelins. The points of the javelins bent easily. So it was difficult for the enemy to pull them out of their shields. In the confusion, the Romans charged, using their swords and daggers. If they were under fire from spears or arrows, the soldiers formed a square and raised their shields above their heads to make a "roof". Protected by this tortoise formation, they advanced further towards the enemy lines.

Keay

Siege Warfare

In the Middle Ages kings and nobles built castles to defend their lands. These strong fortresses had thick stone walls and tall towers. Inside was a stronghold or keep. At the entrance was an iron gate called a portcullis. And there was a drawbridge which could be pulled up to keep out the enemy.

An attack on a castle was called a siege. As the enemy drew near, everyone hurried into the castle. Food and water were stored inside, for a siege might last many weeks.

The attackers surrounded the castle to stop supplies getting in.

Huge "siege engines" hurled rocks and spears. Tunnels were dug beneath the walls. And soldiers climbed up ladders and wooden siege towers.

The defenders fought back by pushing away the ladders with poles and setting fire to the towers. They fired arrows and dropped stones and boiling oil on the enemy. Sometimes the defenders ran out of food and water and surrendered. But often the attackers gave up first and marched away. The age of castles lasted until the cannon was invented. Even the strongest castle walls crumbled under cannon fire.

ballista

mangonel

Protected by a wooden hoarding a castle soldier fires on the enemy.

trebuchet

siege tower

drawbridge

scaling ladder

Crossbow and Longbow

In a medieval battle, the most powerful soldiers were knights. They wore fine metal armor and rode on horseback, charging through the enemy with lances, swords, axes and war hammers. The poorer foot soldiers had no armor. Some carried spears and pikes. Others had to use ordinary farm tools.

The best defense against knights was the bow and arrow. English archers used the longbow, made of yew, which could shoot arrows through steel armor. French archers preferred the crossbow, which fired a short arrow called a bolt (see opposite page).

During the Middle Ages, England and France were often at war. In 1415, King Henry V and his English army fought a famous battle near

the village of Agincourt in France.

The English had only 6,000 men, mostly foot soldiers and archers. The French army was much larger. Expecting an easy victory, the proud French knights jostled for a place in the front as they attacked. Crowded together, they made an easy target for the English bowmen who sheltered behind lines of sharp wooden stakes stuck in the ground.

Many horses were killed as they stumbled over the stakes. And on foot the knights could not move easily in their heavy armor. Many were killed or trampled to death by frightened war horses. When the battle was over, fewer than 500 English soldiers were dead or wounded. But more than 5,000 Frenchmen had lost their lives. Agincourt had proved that the longbow was the best weapon of the Middle Ages.

CROSSBOW

stirrup

bowstring

bolt

trigger

archer loading crossbow

The first guns were cast in iron or bronze, and were very heavy. They fired solid cannon balls.

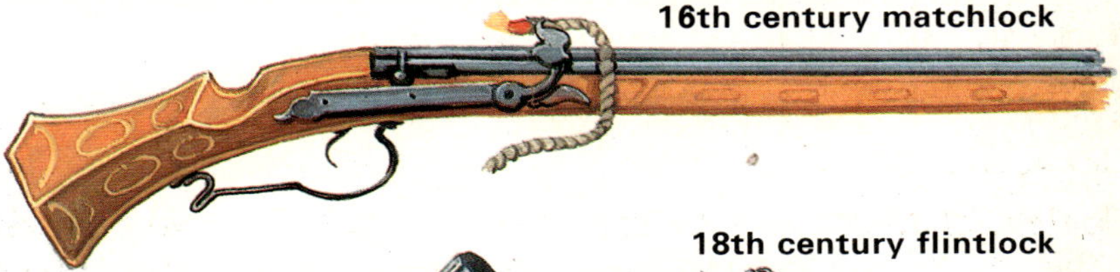

16th century matchlock

18th century flintlock

the Gatling gun, the first successful machine-gun, 1861

loading a 17th century musket

Colt revolver of 1836

modern American police revolver

The Gun

Gunpowder is a mixture of salt-peter, charcoal and sulfur. As long ago as the 12th century, people knew that it could explode violently. The first guns were large hollow tubes made of metal. They were closed at one end and filled with gunpowder. When a flame was put to a small touch-hole, the powder exploded and shot a metal ball or stone out of the mouth of the gun.

Early cannon were not very accurate. Sometimes they blew up, killing their gunners. But the noise, smoke and flames they made frightened the enemy. And cannon balls could knock down the thickest castle walls.

The first handguns were rather like small cannon. The matchlock musket was too heavy to hold without a "rest" and it took a long time to load. When the musketeer squeezed the trigger, a slow-burning match

was touched against the powder in a small pan. This "flash" then set off the main charge.

A better musket, called the flint-lock, was invented in the 18th century. Squeezing the trigger made a flint strike a piece of steel so that a spark fell on to the powder. Later, other explosives were used instead of gunpowder. And the firing system of the gun was improved.

In the 19th century, J. R. Gatling invented a ten-barrel revolving rifle which was used in the American Civil War. Other machine-guns soon followed. The most powerful was the Maxim gun of 1884.

Armies needed guns that fired farther and faster. For greater accuracy, barrels were "rifled" or cut inside with spiral grooves. These spun the bullet, making it fly straighter. And the invention of metal cartridges, each one containing a powder charge and a bullet, made guns easier to load.

The Thin Red Line

Until the 18th century few countries had regular, professional armies. When war broke out, men were called up as soldiers. As soon as peace returned, they went home.

When cannon and muskets replaced bows and arrows, rules of war were drawn up and many regular armies were formed. Rich noblemen formed their own regiments, often dressing their men in handsome uniforms.

Before a battle, the two armies lined up in sight of each other with flags flying and drums beating. Cannon fired and the infantry marched slowly forwards, stopping to fire musket volleys at the enemy. As soon as one side's line was broken, the cavalry charged.

Most battles during the Napoleonic Wars were fought in this way. At the battle of Waterloo in 1815, lines of British infantry in their red uniforms stood fast against the French cavalry. And the "thin red line" became famous.

In the 19th century, Great Britain ruled a huge empire overseas. In battles against the Sikhs and Afghans in India and the Zulus in Africa, the British army's training usually won the day.

The infantry advanced line by line. The first line would fire. Then, as the first reloaded their rifles, the next line would advance and fire. Keeping up a steady fire in this way, the troops advanced until they were close enough to charge the enemy with fixed bayonets.

Many soldiers died in such attacks, particularly when they were ordered to march across open ground against artillery or rifle fire. Their colorful uniforms were easy targets for the enemy. So, by the end of the 19th century, dull khaki uniforms had replaced the bright red coats of the "thin red line."

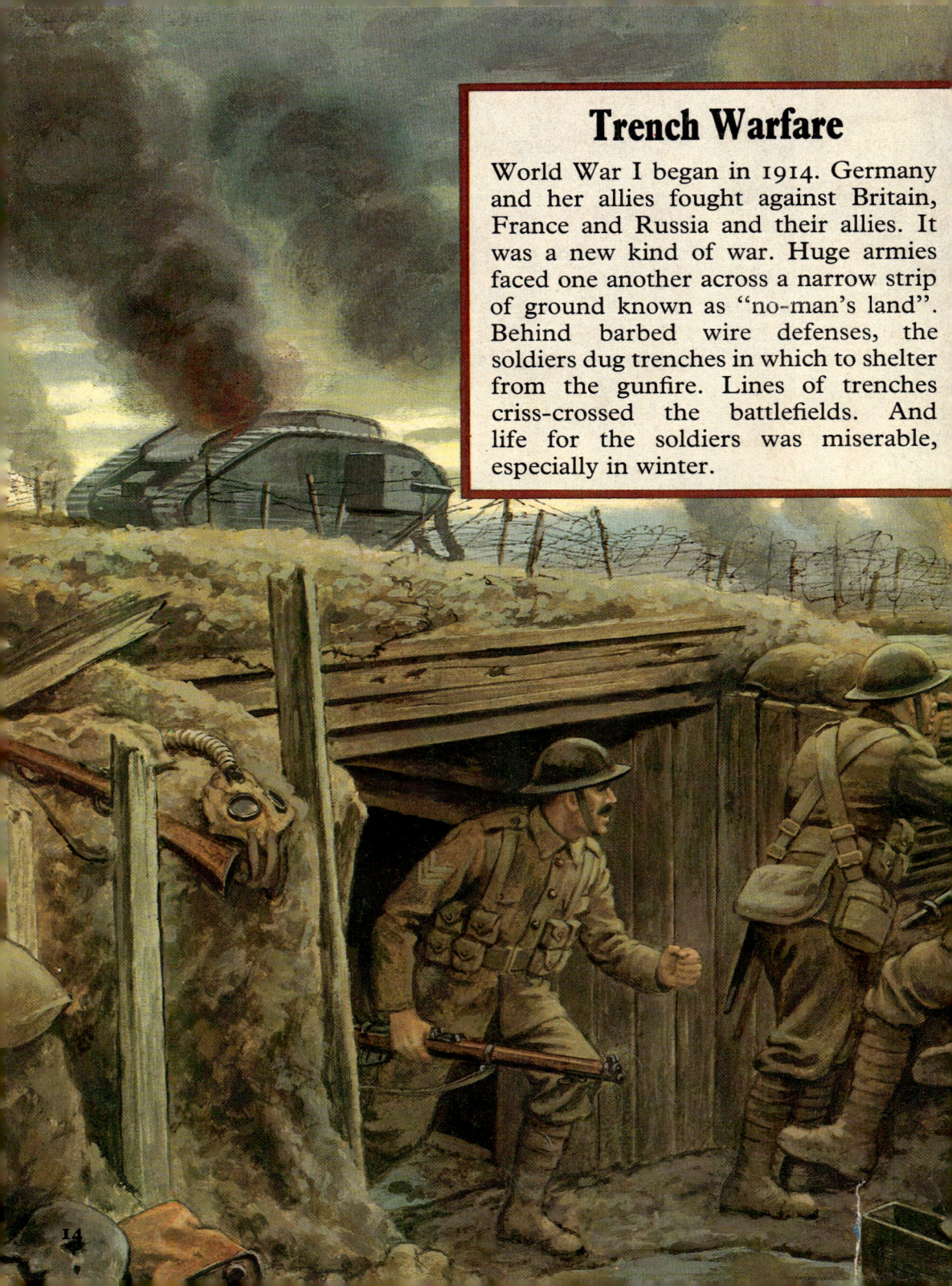

Trench Warfare

World War I began in 1914. Germany and her allies fought against Britain, France and Russia and their allies. It was a new kind of war. Huge armies faced one another across a narrow strip of ground known as "no-man's land". Behind barbed wire defenses, the soldiers dug trenches in which to shelter from the gunfire. Lines of trenches criss-crossed the battlefields. And life for the soldiers was miserable, especially in winter.

Before an attack, heavy guns fired thousands of high explosive shells at the enemy lines. The shells left deep holes everywhere and churned the ground into mud. Then the infantry charged out of the trenches. They wore steel helmets and carried rifles and hand grenades. Often they fought hand-to-hand with bayonets.

After each attack, thousands more soldiers lay dead. Both sides fought bravely, but seldom won more than a few hundred yards of ground.

New weapons, such as poison gas and tanks were used. The quick-firing machine gun had made cavalry out of date. Horses were gradually replaced by armored vehicles and trucks. And for the first time, airplanes flew over the lines.

By 1918, the German armies were worn out. The Allies, helped by fresh American troops, broke through at last, and World War I was over. More than eight million men had lost their lives. Never again would people think of war as an exciting adventure.

British fighters attack German tanks in a desert battle of World War II

Night air-raid in World War II

Tanks and Planes

People thought World War I had been "the war to end all wars". But in 1939 another great war, World War II, began.

In this war, the most deadly weapons on land were tanks. And fighter and bomber planes ruled in the air. The Germans used these weapons in their "blitzkrieg" or "lightning war" attacks. Armored columns drove across country at high speed, supported by aircraft. Soldiers were often dropped by parachute behind the enemy lines.

In North Africa and Russia hundreds of tanks, armored vehicles and guns took part in land battles. The tanks ran on caterpillar tracks to help them cross rough ground. They had powerful guns mounted in turrets and thick steel armor to protect the men inside.

One of the most important battles of World War II was fought in the air. This was the Battle of Britain in 1940. The fighters of the Royal Air Force defeated the attacks of the heavy German bombers, and so stopped Germany from invading Britain.

Both sides used bombers in air raids, killing many people and destroying whole towns. Barrage balloons floating on long cables were one defense. They burst into flames when they were hit. And at night searchlights swept the sky, picking out enemy bombers as targets for anti-aircraft guns. Radar was used to spot bombers and to guide the fast fighters sent up to attack them.

War at Sea

The first sea battles were fought in ancient times. The Persians, Greeks and Romans had warships called galleys with sails and oars. In battle, the ships tried to ram each other. Galley slaves rowed as fast as possible, crashing into enemy ships to damage them so that they sank.

Outside the Mediterranean, the seas were too rough for galleys. In the Middle Ages, some warships looked like floating castles, with raised decks at each end crowded with soldiers.

A great change came with the invention of guns. Handsome wooden galleons tried to sail faster than the enemy and fire "broadsides" from their rows of cannon. In 1588 the faster English ships defeated the large, clumsy galleons of the Spanish Armada. The last great battle between wooden sailing ships, or "men-of-war", was in 1805 at Trafalgar, when the British fleet under Nelson

defeated the French and Spanish. During the 19th century steam engines replace sails and armored battleships, known as "ironclads" appeared. Their guns were mounted in revolving turrets and fired exploding shells.

The biggest naval battle of World War I was Jutland in 1916. Neither side won a clear victory. In World War II, American and Japanese aircraft carriers fought long-range battles in the Pacific, while submarines sank many ships with torpedoes.

**Mushroom cloud
nuclear explosion**

V-1 'flying bomb'

Missile-carrying nuclear submarine

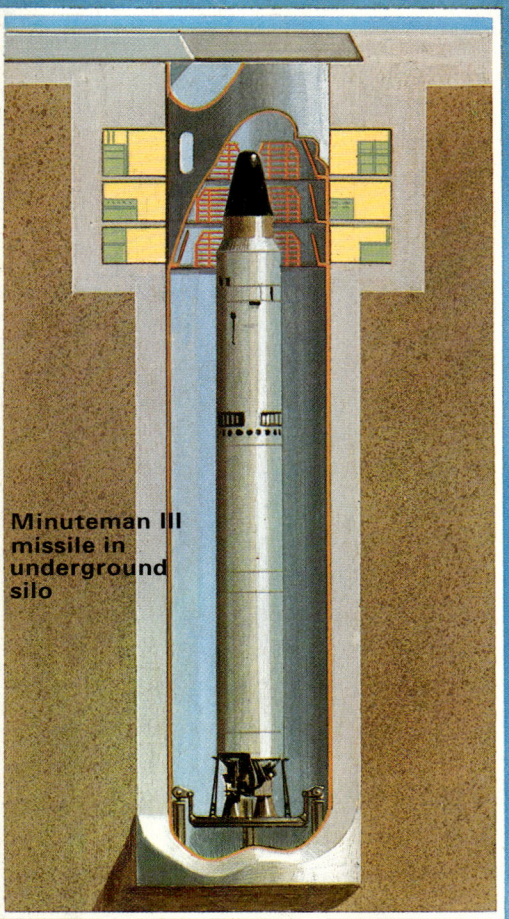
Minuteman III missile in underground silo

To make it more difficult for an enemy to find and destroy them, missiles are hidden underground in concrete silos. They can also be fired from submarines beneath the sea. Nuclear-powered missile-carrying submarines can stay underwater for weeks at a time.

When a nuclear bomb explodes, a huge mushroom cloud rises high into the air. The blast, heat and radioactive fall-out produced by an explosion destroys all life over a huge area.

The Missile Age

Rockets were first used by the Chinese as weapons as well as fireworks. But after guns were invented, rockets were not often used in war until modern times. Today, guided missiles—large rockets carrying nuclear bombs—are the most terrible of all weapons.

The first "flying bomb" was the V-1. Used by Germany in World War II, it was a small pilotless aircraft with a jet engine. Inside it was packed with explosives. After launching, the V-1 flew on until after a set time its motor stopped. Then it fell to earth and exploded.

The V-1 was followed by the V-2, a bigger, faster, rocket-powered missile. After the war, the V-2 was copied by the Americans and the Russians. New rockets were built. Some were used to explore space, others to carry nuclear weapons.

The first atomic bombs, dropped on two Japanese cities in 1945, were carried by aircraft. To carry the much more powerful hydrogen bomb, long-range ballistic missiles were built. These large rockets have several motors. They work in stages and fly so fast that they can cross continents in minutes. The bomb or "warhead" is carried in the nose. Some missiles can carry several warheads, each one guided electronically to a different target.

1

2

3

4

5

6

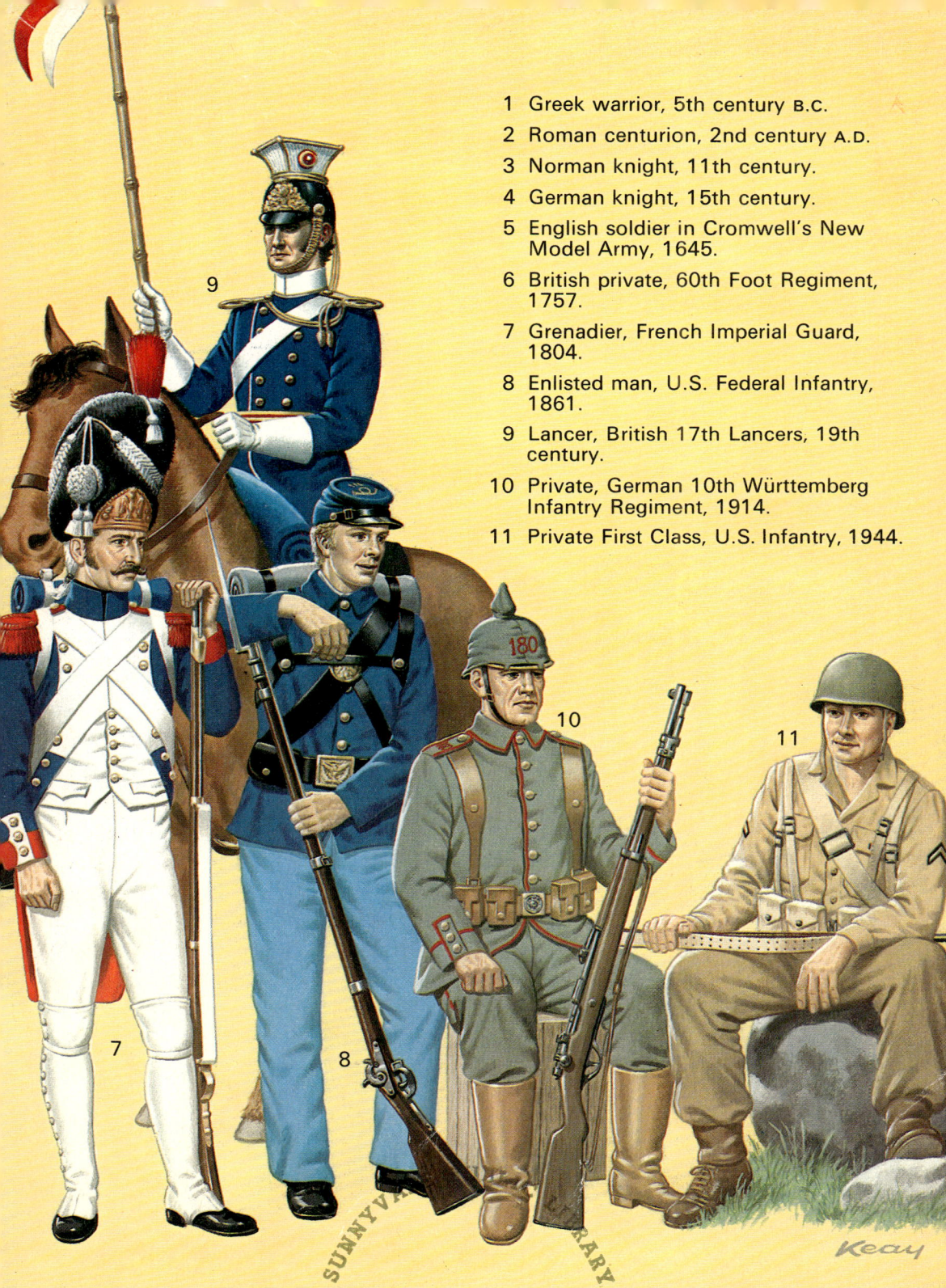

1 Greek warrior, 5th century B.C.

2 Roman centurion, 2nd century A.D.

3 Norman knight, 11th century.

4 German knight, 15th century.

5 English soldier in Cromwell's New Model Army, 1645.

6 British private, 60th Foot Regiment, 1757.

7 Grenadier, French Imperial Guard, 1804.

8 Enlisted man, U.S. Federal Infantry, 1861.

9 Lancer, British 17th Lancers, 19th century.

10 Private, German 10th Württemberg Infantry Regiment, 1914.

11 Private First Class, U.S. Infantry, 1944.